Innovation Africa

Motivational and Inspirational
Stories of Entrepreneurs and
Innovators from Africa

Series I

By

I0476240

Francis Stevens George

&

Thor-Erik Gulliksen

Entrepreneurship is the heart beat of a country, if you do not take care of it the whole system with crumble. Henri Nyakarundi

"Youth entrepreneurs are driving Africa`s growth". Amina Adhan

Innovative people bring new ideas to old formulas. In places such as my country, it seems business people have been going through the same circles and it's about time fresh minds brought something new to the table. Mweemba Ntembe

Africa need people with an extraordinary mind, it needs people who are against dependency syndrome; African needs people that will recognize the plenty of opportunities and transform them into business to advance our economy. Erick Chrispin

Sierra Leone is not an advance country in terms of technology such as robots and all this is why my innovation is unique and it is the first in West Africa. Abioseh Dundas

Companies that do not incorporate innovative ideas, or partner with innovative companies have an expiration date. Henri Nyakarundi

Entrepreneurship is based on real life risk taking experience; not theoretical experience. Entrepreneurs in Africa do not have the requisite materials that will motivate them to take risk. Abdul Karim Kamara

Foreword

We have chosen six stories for the first series of Innovation Africa books. The stories come from Rwanda, Namibia, Sierra Leone, Tanzania and Zambia.

The individuals featured in this book are not only motivated for personal success but for the success of their countries and indeed the entire continent.

The stories of these individuals are truly inspirational; we see individuals that have faced immense challenges in both their personal and business lives; we see individuals who have to conduct business in some the most bureaucratic countries in Africa; and we see individuals who are incredibly motivated to overcome every challenged place in their path.

We asked our entrepreneurs and innovators nineteen questions that reveal their personalities, what drives them and their vision for the future. For all of them, a vision that goes beyond their business to encompass a better world.

For some individuals, their answers are comprehensive, while for others, their answers are less so. This is partly because their business is still in development and partly we do not fully understand the ecosystem in which they operate.

We have done the minimum of editing. What you read are the words and tone of the entrepreneurs and innovators.

Our aim with this book is twofold.

First, we want to share the stories of these individuals as an inspiration to others.

Second, we want others to learn from these individuals. In this regard, we attempted to answer four key questions we believe will contribute to learning. The questions are:

What type of Innovation?

What were the sources of their innovation?

What lessons we can learn; and

What opportunities exist for further development in their business?

We also attempted to answer what, if any, are the environmental impact of their business.

One of the issues in Africa is a lack of adequate innovation systems in many countries. As such, the insights we gain from the answer to these questions will further our understanding of the sources of innovation and more important how these innovations are taken to market.

In conclusion, it is our hope that through these individuals, we can learn and be inspired.

We strongly believe that entrepreneurship is the key for African countries in job creation and leveraging the opportunities of a globalized and connected world.

Through entrepreneurship, economic and social change becomes possible from the bottom up.

Developing countries are increasingly embracing innovation and entrepreneurship as key to their social and economic development, **The World Bank**

Francis Stevens George

Thor-Eirik Gulliksen

Oslo, 2016

Table of Contents

FOREWORD 6

ACKNOWLEDGMENT 10

HENRI NYAKARUNDI 11

    LESSONS LEARNED 26
    TIPS FROM THE AUTHORS.................................30

ABDUL KARIM KAMARA 32

    LESSONS LEARNED 41
    TIPS FROM THE AUTHORS.................................44

GERSON MANGUNDU 45

    LESSONS LEARNED 52
    TIPS FROM THE AUTHORS.................................56

MWEEMBA NTEMBE 57

    LESSONS LEARNED 68
    TIPS FROM THE AUTHORS.................................71

ERICK CHRISPIN 72

    LESSONS LEARNED 84
    TIPS FROM THE AUTHORS.................................86

OSWALD ABIOSEH DUNDAS 87

    LESSONS LEARNED 91
    TIPS FROM THE AUTHORS.................................93

THE AUTHORS...94

    FRANCIS STEVENS GEORGE.............................94
    THOR-ERIK GULLIKSEN 95

TABLE OF INDEX 97

INSPIRING QUOTES 102

Acknowledgment

We wish to thank individuals that contributed to this project.

In their busy schedules, they made time to answer our questions. They also provided valuable input into the several drafts.

We also wish to thank Solomon Roberts of Sensi Tech Hub Sierra Leone, whose assistance with the final formatting was invaluable.

All footnotes are credited to Wikipedia

Henri Nyakarundi

Country: Rwanda

Company: Ared

http://www.a-r-e-d.com

ARED, has developed a mobile solar kiosk in Rwanda which is a one stop shop income generating business solution for people at the BOP[1] level.

Your background. Tell us about your education and most important things you learnt growing up.

----

1 In economics, the bottom of the pyramid is the largest, but poorest socio-economic group. In global terms, this is the 3 billion people who live on less than US$2.50 per day. The phrase "bottom of the pyramid" is used in particular by people developing new models of doing business that deliberately target that demographic, often using new technology. This field is also often referred to as the "Base of the Pyramid" or just the "BoP".

I was born in Kenya but grew up in Burundi, and then moved to Atlanta, USA, in 1996 for University studies. I graduated in 2007 with a computer science degree.

However, to be honest I was not an academic. I tried several times to quit school, but my mother was definitely against it.

I was the typical kid, getting in trouble all the time. I use to believe that there was a short cut to success, but after two years living in America specially when I started living by myself, I started learning about real life;- bills, debts, responsibilities.

My life really changed when my daughter was born. I was 24 with no career and just working part time as a driver in a hotel. It was at this point I started to take life seriously, with a focus on business rather than job/career path.

Deep down business is what I was meant to do. With a mouth to feed, I had to now take it seriously.

The rest as we say is history.

Do you think education in Africa motivates and equips African entrepreneurs?

Absolutely not!

The educational system in Africa produces job seekers and not job creators. We need a total change of the school system where real entrepreneurs teach classes.

We need to teach students about paying bills, savings, budgeting; in short, real life skills. Instead, we focus on theories such as geography, foreign history stuff that we can learn in our personal time.

In addition, the educational tenure is too long; you finish secondary school, then we go to university where you spend two years learning about subjects called refreshing courses.

I believe these subjects do not prepare students for the real world. This is a handicap to them because an individual that is not prepared, will most likely become unemployed.

Where did you get the idea for your business?

Like most ideas, it came from a personal experience. Every time I traveled on vacation to Burundi, I was having a problem keeping my cell phone charged. As a result, I thought about a device that could help people charge their phone while they are outside of their homes and offices.

I did some research and could not find anything that fitted my need. I then decided to develop something.

The technology for the first prototype took 4 years to develop. The initial idea was to lease the kiosk and make money on branding.

As with most ideas, it has evolved to the point where we are now laying the ground to provide more intelligent services such as internet hot spot, and digital advertisement.

How does your business model work?

Our Company, ARED, has developed a mobile solar kiosk in Rwanda which is a one stop shop income generating business solution for people at the BOP level.

We provide services such as charging small electronics, mobile money, and internet hotspot using a low cost franchise business model.

Our goal is to empower people at the base of the pyramid through entrepreneurship.

We offer a low cost business, but to maximize the revenue of our franchisees we take care of all the back end such as negotiating with key partners, adding new services and training the entrepreneurs on key points.

The job of the franchisee is to focus on the customer. This is the best model we found to increase the franchisee rate of success.

How do you attract customers?

Our mobile solar kiosk is an outdoor product, and we make sure we position ourselves in high traffic areas such as bus stop, market place, health center and other high traffic spots.

Branding the kiosk with its unique look attract customer readily.

Our kiosk based in Rwanda average around 30 customers a day. We plan to increase that number when we bring WIFI internet hotspot to our kiosks.

Our goal is to create a one stop service center for any electronic voucher[1] that exist in that specific market.

What is the innovation in your business?

The innovation is both the mobile solar kiosk platform and our business model.

Mobile type business is the future. Brick and mortar business are expensive and low income people usually cannot afford those type of businesses.

Mobility eliminates that problem, and lowers the cost of doing business as no rent is paid when your kiosk is on wheels.

We also added a solar system that allows our franchisees not only to charge any type of electronics but also to operate their business.

The franchisee sell all services electronically using a tablet or smart phone. Services include ewasa, airtime, and mobile money.

They are able to sell these services electronically as they can charge their POS[2] - in this case, a tablet or smart phone- in the kiosk through a solar panel.

All the services sold in the kiosk has been added and negotiated by ARED.

To really add more value, we developed a training program to truly empower the people working in the kiosk. We train them on customer service- such as how to get and keep a customer. We also train then in some the most basic business skills, and even taxes.

The combination of the two systems maximizes the success rate of our franchisees. Our goal is to create an income generating platform that is low cost but maximize their income potential with all the services we offer.

---

2 The point of sale (POS) is the time and place where a retail transaction is completed. It is the point at which a customer makes a payment to the merchant in exchange for goods or after provision of a service. At the point of sale, the merchant would prepare an invoice for the customer (which may be a cash register printout) or otherwise calculate the amount owed by the customer and provide options for the customer to make payment. After receiving payment, the merchant will also normally issue a receipt for the transaction. Usually the receipt is printed, but it is increasingly being dispensed electronically.

What is the most fulfilling and rewarding part of what you have been doing?

I designed the kiosk and the business model to really impact the people that need or are looking for an opportunity to be in business but cannot afford to start a traditional business.

We have impacted 25 people so far. Of these, 8 (just over 30%) are women and 70% men. 5% of the franchisees that have a disability.

One of our franchisees has already added a second kiosk. This is how business should be, helping others that will in return help our business. It is a true win-win situation.

Being in business for over 15 years, I use to believe that having money was the key to happiness. However, time and experience has taught me that a true positive contribution to another human being is my true purpose and money should be used as a tool to achieve something greater than ourselves.

What challenges have you faced during your time as an entrepreneur?

Entrepreneurship is synonym for challenges. You do not start a business if you are not a problem solver.

As such, I do not call them challenges but opportunity to learn. Your mind set in business has to be different from a traditional mindset.

If you look at something in a different light it will be much easier to solve it. But to get back to the question, the main challenge has been access to funding, specially grant for Research and Development (R&D).

I realized that in Africa, we are so behind in developing technology because Governments do not spend enough resources on R&D.

Further challenges were, finding manufacturing companies in Africa that are willing to work with SME's; the lack of appetite by a larger company to partner with smaller but innovative companies; the fragmentation of the Africa market; high taxes that cripples SME's; and finding affordable qualified employees.

I can go on and on but this is why I am in business; you only learn through challenges and success is our best reward.

What are the three most important things you had done for your success?

Success to me is like a recipe; it requires several ingredients to make a meal taste good.

To me I would pick *hard work*, *focus*, and *persistence*.

Has anyone mentored or inspired you?

The best mentor is Life itself.

However I spend a lot of time reading books like "Think and Grow Rich[3] ", "Unstoppable[4] " that give you a small insight of what it takes to be successful.

---

[3] Think and Grow Rich was written in 1937 by Napoleon Hill and is a personal development and self-improvement book. Hill was inspired by a suggestion from Scottish- American business magnate and philanthropist Andrew Carnegie. While the book's title implies that the it deals with how to attain monetary wealth, the author explains that the philosophy taught in the book can be used to help people succeed in all lines of work, to do and be almost anything they want.

[4] From Amazon: Being unstoppable is about believing and achieving. It's about having faith in yourself, your talents, your purpose. And most of all, in God's great love and His divine plan for your life. Millions around the world recognize the smiling face and inspirational messages of Nick Vujicic. Born without arms or legs, Nick has not allowed his physical challenges to keep him from enjoying great adventures, a fulfilling and meaningful career, and loving relation-ships. Nick has overcome trials and hardships by focusing on the promises that he was created for a unique and specific purpose that his life has value and is a gift to others, and that even though he may endure hardships, God is always present and in control. Nick credits his success to the power that is unleashed when we put our faith into action.

I am a self-taught entrepreneur which is really the best and the worse way to be an entrepreneur. Best because you really learn the hard way. However, worse because you make more mistake than someone who has a good mentor that can really show you how to avoid them.

How can you translate your experience into mentoring others?

I do it sometimes, if I am asked but at this time is hard because I am so busy. I do my best to help, but I require that the person is already in business.

I have notice a lot of young people are scared of asking for help or for mentorship. Sometimes you get people that are still undecided about taking the jump to become an entrepreneur.

This is a big no-no in my book. I do not want to waste time on such people. Procrastination and fear is a killer for a potential entrepreneur.

It is a hard decision, but you'll never know the end result until you do it and stick to it no matter what.

Which African Entrepreneurs inspire you and why?

I always amazed by young entrepreneurs in their early 20's showing laser focus mindset and actually achieving big things like Verone Mankou[5] .

Verone developed a tablet and is competing with the big companies in the game. And there are many more "Verones" on the continent.

What three advice do you have for other entrepreneurs?

First, prepare your mind that your entrepreneurial journey will be hard, it's a mental game.

Do not fall for the glamour shown on the media of people turning a profitable company in less than 2 years. It

---

5 He is seen as the new "Steve Jobs of Africa." According to the famous Forbes magazine, he is listed among the 30 Top "best African entrepreneurs less than 30 years of age." At 27 years old, Vérone Mankou is one of the young prodigies of the net in Africa! Since 2009, he has been the chairman and managing director of the Congolese company, VMK ("Vou Mou Ka",In December 2011, Vérone Mankou launched the first African "tablet computer", the Way-C. In 2012, he added the first African smartphone, Elikia ("Hope" in Lingala, the native language in Congo). The basic version of Elikia is called "Elikia Mokè.

only happens to a few of them. Most of us actually will be doing a marathon.

Second, make as many mistakes as you can especially if you have an innovative product or service, and learn from your mistakes so you can adapt and adjust to always improve your business model and find new revenue streams.

Business of today is in constant evolution, do not ever believe you have an edge, new technology come into market all the time, new ideas are becoming a commodity so never stop learning and improving.

Last but not least, the most important and my favorite one is persistence. Never, ever give up! Entrepreneurship is a painful journey, but only the ones that set their mind up to never give up succeed is that simple.

Quitters never win and winners never quit.

What prospects do you see for your company?

I see this company to be a USD 50 million company and have a presence in most countries in Africa and South America.

We are moving for a hardware technology to include a software component that will lay the ground for more intelligent services.

How important is innovation and innovators like you for the development of Africa?

Innovation is key to solving some of the biggest challenges countries face around the world.

These range from global warming, access to clean water, drug development, agricultural productivity and not least unemployment; in particular youth unemployment-

It is also the key for large companies to stay relevant.

Companies that do not incorporate innovative ideas, or partner with innovative companies have an expiration date.

Telecom is the perfect example, you can tell the difference between which telecoms adopt innovative ideas and the ones that do not.

Unfortunately, in Africa innovation is still new, misunderstood and not well accepted yet.

We want to keep the status quo, and because of that we keep trailing when it comes to keeping up with technology, developing our own technology and solving our problem using local talent and solutions.

What industries, and lucrative business areas do you think will provide future business opportunities for African entrepreneurs?

Definitely the agricultural sector. With a population growing so fast, and global warming threatening our existence, new innovative ways to grow food (such as vertical solution or indoor solutions), and process food, distribute food are the next big opportunities.

For example, 30% of our food goes to waste because of poor distribution channel. A solution is really needed in that space.

Also the internet of things (IoT)[6] is really going to bring more value to any company to really know what's going on with their product and how's customer use them. Companies that now have real time analytics.

The energy sector, renewable energy is offering exciting and new possibilities. The technology needs to improve and get business models need to become more innovative.

_____

[6] The Internet of Things refers to the networking of physical objects through the use of embedded sensors, actuators, and other devices that can collect or transmit information about the objects. According to Gartner, Inc. (a technology research and advisory corporation), there will be nearly 26 billion devices on the Internet of Things by 2020. The data amassed from these devices can then be analyzed to optimize products, services, and operations. The interconnection of these embedded devices (including smart objects), is expected to usher in automation in nearly all fields, while also enabling advanced applications like a Smart Grid, and expanding to the areas such as smart cities.

The opportunities are huge when one considers that less than 25% of the total population of Africa have access to electricity.

What support do you think African governments must give to young African innovators and entrepreneurs?

Well the job of the Government is to play the role of a referee, making sure the laws protect us, ease on taxes, facilitate access to finances and also allow some of the tender to be allocated to SME's.

Entrepreneurship is the heart beat of a country, if you do not take care of it the whole system with crumble.

If you were President, what would you do or what would you change to encourage growth in entrepreneurship?

I would first facilitate the creation of venture capital/angel investors by offering tax incentives to promote local investor in investing in local companies.

Following this I will then put in place grant programs in each department of government, especially those that need to promote local R&D and enable the development of local technology to solve local problems.

We need tax incentives, grant programs for R&D, 3 year of tax free for start up`s and at last push big companies to use some percentage in local SME.

I would also offer a 3-year tax free environment for startups in key sectors.

Finally, push for a law that forces larger companies that receive government tenders to have a percentage of that tender to go to a local Small Medium Enterprise.

Government spends way too much money on foreign expertise, that bring their own staff and as a country we do not benefit much. To strengthen an economy, we need to strengthen the private sector. We should have more (local companies that do mining, and build roads.

Lessons Learned

What type of innovation?

Henri's innovation comes under product system innovation. Such innovation is defined in how separate or individual products and services are connected or packaged to create a new and dynamic offering.

The key is to look for connections between these sometimes separate products or services. Henri, through his research has done just this.

According to the theory, through integration, interoperability and modularity, one can build the new offering. Since one is connecting separate products and services, an eco-system is soon created through which one can continue to offer new services and products to your customers.

This is exactly what Henri has done.

Henri wanted to "help people charge their phone while they are outside their homes or offices".

Until he created his product, the majority of people could only charge their phones when they were either at home or at their offices. His product has created value by making it possible to charge ones phones outside the office or their home.

He has done this by taking a normal kiosk and adding solar charging capabilities to this. From this base product, several other products and services are now offered from the same.

The eco-system he is building is offering scalable value to both his franchisees and their customers.

To continue with his innovation, Henri also identified the need to train his franchise in basic business skills.

As he puts it, "But to really add more value, we developed a training program to truly empower the people working on the kiosk. We train them about customer service, taxes and how to maintain customers by giving some incentives.

The combination of the two systems maximizes the success rate of our franchisees".

The Source of his Innovation

The source of Henri's innovation is stems from both a process need and his own personal need.

He found it a challenge to charge his mobile phone when he was outside his office or home. It was this frustration that led him to identify the process that needs to be changed, if he was to meet the challenge of charging his mobile phone while outside his home or office.

The process of charging one's mobile phone was limited to either ones office or home. Henri's mobile solar kiosk has now remove that limitation.

What makes Henri's experience unique is that he actually decided to do something about his frustration. These are his own words;

"Like most idea it came from a personal experience. Every time I traveled on vacation in Burundi I was having problem keeping my cell phone charged.

So I thought about a device that could help people charge their phone while their outside their home or offices. I did some research and could not find anything that fitted my need so I decided to develop something."

The mobile phone operator or even handset maker did not identify this as a potential business, which makes Henri's idea all the more valuable.

What opportunities for further ideas or development of a new business?

Product system innovation often leads to the development of a technological eco system.

"Technology ecosystems are product platforms defined by core components made by the platform owner and complemented by applications made by autonomous companies in the periphery".

They are not just charging mobile phones, but charging small electronics, sending mobile money, and internet hotspot using a low cost franchise business model.

His goal as he puts it is to "create a one stop service center for any electronic voucher that exist in that specific market and digital services".

What, if any, is environmental impact of his innovation or business?

Henri uses solar energy to charge various devices.

Therefore, going solar will have a positive impact on the environment as it eliminates diesel/gasoline use, thus reducing greenhouse gases.

What are the lessons we can take from Henri?

This is a classical entrepreneur story. Henri had a problem for which he could not readily find a solution.

After some research he decided to develop his own solution.

Across the world, we find similar stories.

We find the social responsibility embedded in his business idea quite admirable and one that holds important lessons for his success.

Perhaps the best "lessons learned" is Henri's life philosophy.

In particular how he sees challenges rather than problems, and spotting an opportunity in problems.

He calls them "opportunities to learn".

Tips from the Authors

Henri natural talents has got him very far in the development of his business. Henri could benefit from a mentor, especially when expanding his business to other countries and increasing his offering.

As with most franchises, success depends on maintaining the same standard across franchisees. This normally calls for a careful selection of suppliers of products and services in order to maintain the same standard.

More critical is the selections of the franchisees. A tip from us is that Henri brings all the franchisees together regularly to exchange ideas and to build the "family feeling".

In some of these gatherings the suppliers can also participate. We believe this would increase the chances of maintaining the same standard for the franchisees, and ultimately continue the success.

Abdul Karim Kamara

Country: Sierra Leone

Company: Envirotech General Services Limited

Turns plastic waste into tiles to use as building material

Your background. Tell us about your education and most important things you learnt growing up.

My name is Abdul Karim Kamara and I am a Sierra Leonean. I have a Diploma in Business Studies from Milton Margai College of Education Science and Technology (MMCE&T) Goderich campus, Freetown.

I am also a graduate from the University of Makeni (UNIMAK) with a bachelor of science (BSc) in Human Resources Management (HRM).

I am currently pursuing my Masters in Business Administration (MBA) in global business and sustainable entrepreneurship at the Catholic School of Business in Milan (Italy) and University of Makeni (UNIMAK) Makeni, Sierra Leone.

Some of the key things I learnt growing up are discipline, challenge, perseverance, and focus. I also learn to prepare to take reasonable risk.

Last but not least, is willingness and be open for learning every day.

Do you think education in Africa motivates and equips African entrepreneurs?

I do not think education in Africa motivates and equips African entrepreneurs.

The reason is until recently, education in Africa was too much of "bookishness" and less of real life issues.

In Africa, we focus on the conventional way of learning by going to university to study business studies, reading educational discipline books written by other people without doing it practically. African education is more theory than practice.

> *Entrepreneurship is based on real life risk taking experience; not theoretical experience. Entrepreneurs in Africa do not have the requisite materials that will motivate them to take risk.*

As such, we have very little entrepreneurs in Africa as compared to other continents.

For example, our engineers are merely replicating theories propounded long time ago and do not have the necessary skills to commercialize their disciplines.

As such, a majority of them end up being employees instead of employers or entrepreneurs.

Where did you get the idea for your business?

I have had a long quest to do business since I was in secondary school. When I was in high school, I was a member of one of the most outstanding youth groups in Bombali District[7].

As a youth group we engaged in several activities in the district including the usual end of month city cleaning. As a group we took a leading role in the cleaning exercise.

After the civil war[8], I have been thinking how I could make money though waste management. Before and after

---

7 Bombali District is a district in the Northern Province of Sierra Leone. Its capital and largest city is Makeni, which is also the largest city in the north. The other major towns in the district include Kamakwie, Kamabai, Karina and Binkolo. Bombali is the second largest district in Sierra Leone in geographical area (after Koinadugu District) and the second most populous district in the North, after Port Loko District. The population of Bombali district as of 2010 is 434,319.

8 The Sierra Leone Civil War (1991-2002) began on 23 March 1991 when the Revolutionary United Front (RUF), with support from the special forces of Charles Taylor's National Patriotic Front of Liberia (NPFL), intervened in Sierra Leone in an attempt to overthrow the

the war I was a volunteer with the Makeni Union of Youth Groups (MUYOG)

Sometime in 2014, I was watching a TV show which was discussing plastic waste. The TV show was discussing plastic waste recycling in Niger.

This immediately reactivated my interest in waste management.

Fortunately, the MBA program[9] was launched at UNIMAK and I applied for the course with plastic waste recycling as my business idea which has earned me a full scholarship.

How does your business model work?

I buy plastic waste from people who collect them from the streets. The plastic is collected by young people who will bring them to our production site.

When the plastics are in my warehouse, I pay freelancers to sort the plastics out and bag them for onward production.

Joseph Momoh government. The resulting civil war lasted 11 years, enveloped the country, and left over 50,000 dead.

9 The MBA course was launched in 2013 at a degree awarding ceremony at the UNIMAK campus.

The next step is that the plastics are melted into complete liquid in a big container.

After the plastic have been melted, sand is then poured into the liquid plastic and then stir for some time and the mixture is then poured into different shapes of moles to give a desired shape.

How do you attract customers?

I attract customers through radio and TV advertisement; through business exhibitions/ trade fairs; through the distribution of product/business leaflets, fliers, brochures, and through one to one marketing.

What is the innovation in your business?

Turning plastic waste into pavement tiles or to put it another way turning waste into cash!

What is the most fulfilling and rewarding part of what you have been doing?

The most rewarding part of what I am doing is the day I did the first sales and the pavement tiles where placed on a customer's site.

Another rewarding moment was the day I paid my staff for their service; I felt fulfilled. I felt I have impacted some homes through this business.

What challenges have you faced during your time as an entrepreneur?

Capital has always been my major challenge since the inception of my business.

What are the three most important things you had done for your success?

The three most important thing I have done for my success are, believe in my business and determined to achieve my goal; passion for my business and resilience and focus and discipline

Has anyone mentored you?

No one has mentored me. However, the MBA secretariat team at UNIMAK and Rev. Fr. Benjamin Sesay have always encourage me to stay focus and be resilient.

How can you translate your experience into mentoring others?

I think my experience is a valuable one because it is real life experience. I have felt what it means to be an entrepreneur, especially when starting with nothing.

However, with belief, determination, passion and hope, I have come far. I can use my real life experience to mentor other entrepreneurs or would be.

Which African Entrepreneurs inspire you and why?

Ashish Thakar[10] is one African entrepreneur that inspires me most because of his determination and resilience and believes in his dream. He challenged his parents even when they don't think doing business at that particular time was the right decision.

He traded his education for business and like I said, because of his determination, belief and resilience, he was able to break through.

What three advice do you have for other entrepreneurs?

Know the problem you want to solve; be focus, determined, discipline and have passion, resilience and challenge yourself to take the risk.

---

10 Ashish J. Thakkar is a British businessman and entrepreneur of Indian descent. He is the founder of Mara Group and Mara Foundation, and he is a co-founder of Atlas Mara. Thakkar was born in the United Kingdom, but he moved to East Africa as a teen-ager before founding Mara Group, a Pan-African conglomerate, at the age of 15. Mara Group's operations and investments span 22 African countries. He is the author of The Lion Awakes: Adventures in Africa's Economic Miracle.Thakkar is a member of the World Economic Forum's Young Global Leaders, and was featured on Fortune Magazine's list of the top "40 Under 40" in 2013. He was awarded the Base Leadership Award at the 2014 MTV Africa Music Awards event.

What prospects do you see for your company?

I see my business to be a ground breaking business that will create other subsidiary businesses.

I see my business has the potential to grow in Africa because plastic is being used all over Africa and the attitude towards plastic waste almost cut across Africa.

A company that has the potential to produce different products from plastic and sand.

What industries, and lucrative business areas do you think will provide future business opportunities for African entrepreneurs?

Africa has a huge potential for tourism. The tourism industry is a lucrative industry in Africa that has not been exhaustively tapped into or utilized. This is actually the case in my own country, Sierra Leone.

Another potential industry for investment in Africa is renewable energy. In most African countries, governments are the main producers of energy and most government does not have the capacity to produce adequate, effective and efficient energy to serve its people.

Rural electricity supply has been a serious challenge for African countries.

Agriculture is another potential for investment in Africa. We have a vast virgin land in Africa that has not been utilized or have been underutilized or poorly utilized.

How important is innovation and innovators like you for the development of Africa?

Africa needs innovative solutions to its problems. Innovators like me are important in Africa because we solve real day to day problems in an African way such as environmental, agriculture, green or renewable energy etc.

We also create employment.

Innovators like me is a new revolution to todays' world.

What support do you think African governments must give to young African innovators and entrepreneurs?

The support African government should give to young African innovators is training, conducive business environment, subsidies and starting or seed capital, which is a key to the challenges or problems of African innovators or entrepreneurs.

If you were President, what would you do or what would you change to encourage growth in entrepreneurship?

If I were the President of Sierra Leone, I would establish structures that would make Sierra Leonean entrepreneurs establish businesses easily, access seed capital easily without much bottleneck, and also provide technical support to them.

Lessons Learned

What type of Innovation?

Abdul's business reflects the change in perception towards plastic waste and recycling of such waste. This is also known as paradigm-based innovations.

Secondly, he has created a new business altogether.

The change in perception is that we now see recycling plastic waste as a viable business. On a higher level, our perception of the need to protect our environment has changed.

We now recognized that recycling plastic is good for our environment, in addition to other environmentally friendly practices.

Due this change in perception, both locally and globally, we see a paradigm shift too.

This is why we can also classify Abdul Karim's innovation under paradigm based innovation.

He turns plastic waste into pavement tiles, which his customers are ready to buy because of a change in their perception about the environment.

Added to the above, this is an entirely new business in Sierra Leone.

The Source of his Innovation

The source of his innovation is twofold. The first is the advances in technology and knowledge in processing and recycling waste.

The second was his membership and activities in a youth group that was cleaning the streets in his town.

Motivated by wanting to make money, he started to think about what he could do with plastic waste.

He saw a change in business (green is good), as a result of a paradigm shift which now recognizes the need for recycling.

Further, he saw a TV program in which the ideas he had were actually been implemented in another African country.

What opportunities for further ideas or development of a new business?

There is clearly a huge potential for Abdul Karim Kamara's business to scale. There are opportunities to tie in stake holders in various parts of the supply chain.

As technological advances are made and his revenue grows, it could open opportunities for more products to be produced.

We see an opportunity for the people that collect the plastic bottles to create their own business and become part of Abdul's ecosystem.

What, if any, is environmental impact of their innovation or business

Without a doubt, Abdul Karim's project has major environmental implications.

Plastic waste is a huge environmental problem globally. In Sierra Leone and in probably other African countries, more than 70% of plastic waste is landfilled.

This means they are not recycled resulting in loss of energy and process raw materials.

Abdul Karim is a pioneer in Sierra Leone by turning plastic waste into pavement tiles.

In the final analysis, through his business he is saving landfill space.

What lessons can we take from Abdul Karim Kamara?

One of the most important lessons is how your passion can be turned into a viable business. As a member of a youth group, Abdul had a passion for cleaning his regional city of Makeni.

It was this passion that lead him to find a way to "make money" from plastic waste.

Tips from the Authors

Abdul needs to find international partners to scale up his business. The partners could be technological, investors or in the construction business.

A mentor within the same branch or similar could help him find good partners. One of the most important aspect when starting a business is to streamline the business and make it ready to scale up.

To have a mentor within the same branch will not only help him to streamline and ready for upscale, but also focus, prioritizing and to get even more motivated.

Gerson Mangundu

Country: Namibia

Company: Namhook

http://www.namhook.com

Namhook is Namibia`s first social network

Your background. Tell us about your education and most important things you learnt growing up.

Well, I was born on the 9th of February 1993 in Kavango region, Namibia.

I started school in 1999, attending Bagani combined school and Max Makushe senior secondary school.

I was one of the top 10 students in the whole country in 2010 grade 12 final exams. After high school, I went to the University of Namibia where I studied civil engineering.

After one year I was granted a scholarship to study Informational Technology in Cuba and that's where I found my company Namhook.

My love for entrepreneurship started at a young age. When I was 18 years old, I had the idea to come up with my own social network for my country.

I saw that there was a need for such a social network that as this could also be combined with a business platform which will help entrepreneurs and the public at large.

Do you think education in Africa motivates and equips African entrepreneurs?

Yes of course, I went through it, it made me who I am today.

Where did you get the idea for your business?

I came up with the idea because I saw there was a need for a social network for my country and also it could be a very good business opportunity since no one has it yet.

I spotted an opportunity. I refuse to start a business which already exists.

My philosophy is "start something fresh and conquer everybody".

Even if someone tries to copy your idea later, your company has already grown and it will be impossible to defeat you.

How does your business model work?

We get revenue from advert campaigns, Listings, commissions from online shopping, music selling and we are monetizing the mobile apps too.

How do you attract customers?

We have attracted customers through positive media coverage and basically due to the exciting features which the social network offers; the public in general enjoy the free services we offer.

Further, the fact that entrepreneurs can market their products on our network, has made us attractive.

What is the innovation in your business?

Being the first one in Namibia and Africa at large to develop a social network.

What challenges have you faced during your time as an entrepreneur?

The most challenging part is starting a business, making an idea to work is not easy especially when you don't have enough funding.

There are times when you will be afraid to invest into an idea because you have mixed feelings of it turning out to be a failure.

In business you always have to risk the little you have.

---

*Scared money don't make
any money.*

What are the three most important things you had done for your success?

Believing in myself was very important; I never stopped trying, and even though I went through obstacles I never stopped trying my best.

Has anyone mentored or inspired you?

Never had a mentor.

How can you translate your experience into mentoring others?

I really don't have a lot of experience in business right now, I'm just an innovator. I do not feel sufficiently experienced to mentor others yet.

Which African Entrepreneurs inspire you and why?

I have not been following a lot of them actually, but I can say the business mogul, Knowledge Katti[11] from Namibia is doing it big.

In fact, after I completed my grade 12, Knowledge Katti gave me a scholarship under his Knowledge Foundation scholarship and he does that like every year helping students.

What three advice do you have for other entrepreneurs?

When opportunity knocks you better open the door; Focus on your dreams and forget about the negative thoughts and do a proper research on a project you are to work on.

---

[11] Knowledge Katti was born and bred at the harbour town Walvis Bay, Namibia's main port, where he also attended completed high school. He has consistently been one of the top students throughout his academic life. He completed a Bachelor of Commerce Degree at the University of Namibia (UNAM), with Economics, Accounting and Auditing as majors subjects. As a way to give back to the country and community that helped shape him, Knowledge Katti established The Knowledge Foundations in 2008.

What prospects do you see for your company?

I see Namhook growing into something bigger than I thought of.

The idea was to have a national social network but since the website went public I have received requests from people from other African countries to make it a continent-wide service. The plan right now is to get all the Namibians sign-up and after that we will conquer the whole Africa.

This is the best network; yes, I can say that with confidence.

No other social network gets close to Namhook.

Namhook got a lot of amazing features so that makes it the best.

How important is innovation and innovators like you for the development of Africa?

It's pretty awesome to come up with something which did not exist yet, it's very important for the development of our continent; we should not only depend on the developed countries.

We need to start doing things ourselves. I am not happy with the current situation of Africa as we depend on foreign countries for almost everything.

What industries and lucrative business areas do you think will provide future business opportunities for African entrepreneurs?

Business opportunities are in technology. If you do a bit of research you will realize that most of the African entrepreneurs are actually investing in real estate. They don't concentrate a lot on technology.

Perhaps because of the complexity which is involved in technology related businesses. However, everything is possible.

People who want to start a new good unique business should first travel out of Africa to the more developed countries.

In such countries one has an opportunity to study new technologies and processes. One also can find services and products that are much needed in Africa.

Africa has a lot of business opportunities but people seem to be reluctant to act.

What support do you think African governments must give to young African innovators and entrepreneurs?

I think the governments should support innovators and young entrepreneurs financially as soon as they start working on their projects to help them emerge rapidly.

Investors can be hard to find sometimes because they don't actually invest into ideas or a business which just started as they want to be sure that the company has started making money.

Therefore African Governments should support young entrepreneurs with seed capital.

If you were President, what would you do or what would you change to encourage growth in entrepreneurship?

If I was President, I will encourage entrepreneurship in my country.

It's the only key to success. We all know that we cannot get rich from our salaries.

I would make sure that there is always funding available for young entrepreneurs and innovators.

Lessons Learned

What type of innovation?

Namhook is a good example of new product innovation. Gerson was already determined from a young age to create something that did not exist.

He identified a need and created a service to meet that need. As he puts it "I came up with the idea because I saw there was a need for a social network for my country and also it could be a very good business opportunity since no one has it yet, it's about opportunities."

Indeed he is the first in his country to create a social network.

The Source of his Innovation

The source of his innovation is a combination of demographic and market changes. There are already global social networks, but creating a local one requires the right demographic and market conditions. Income levels, technology penetration where factors in his innovation.

We can also add his desire and determination to create something new in his country.

We found an interesting point Gerson made regarding the sources of innovation. The point is whether, entrepreneurs need to travel overseas and pick ideas from other countries and bring them back home.

This is what Gerson said, "People who want to start a new good unique business should first travel out of Africa to the more developed countries.

In such countries one has an opportunity to study new technologies and processes. Often times, one also can find services and products that are much needed in Africa.

Africa has a lot of business opportunities but people seem to be reluctant to act."

The authors strongly believe that the sources of innovation lies within individual countries in Africa. It may help one to travel abroad and see solutions that could be implemented in their countries.

However, identifying the need; identifying industry and market changes; studying demographic changes; meeting the unexpected, are factors that are local to a particular country or region.

Indeed, as Gerson said when asked on the importance of Innovation for Africa. He replied, "It's pretty awesome to come up with something which did not exist yet, it's very important for the development of our continent, we should not only depend on the developed countries.

We need to start doing things ourselves. I am not happy with the current situation of Africa as we depend on foreign countries in almost everything."

What opportunities for further ideas or development of a new business?

As with other social networks, we see building value added services around the core product/service will attract and retain more users.

We also see cross platform integration and connection with mobile devices as critical to making Namhook more present in their user's life.

We also believe that a robust social strategy should be part of the overall growth strategy. A social strategy is a combination of content creation, content curation, creativity, and organization.

This opens opportunities for other entrepreneurs and innovators to build applications and services for Namhook.

What lessons can we take from Gerson?

Gerson is young and ambitious. You may find some of his words smack of arrogance, but it's precisely why we like him!

It is such attitude and indeed arrogance that is needed to balance the all too often timid approach in some countries.

In today's fast changing world, we need young men like Gerson that wants to start something new and defend his position through a growth strategy that would be hard to beat by his competitors.

As with Henri Nyakarundi, Gerson identified a need and researched why that need was not been fulfilled.

If it becomes clear you can create value, then go for it.

Tips from the Authors

We believe that Namhook should continue to build sticky services around the business platform.

Namhook should also look for partnerships and alliances with companies that have or are developing products and services that are complimentary to Namhook's offering.

Finally, we believe that he could do with a mentor. He is ambitious, believes himself, but he is young.

This is where a mentor will be of value to him.

Mweemba Ntembe

Country: Zambia

Company: The Panjiia Company

Brings Zambian farmers together as a cooperative, enabling them to their produce together and trade to buyers in Asia, Europe and America

Your background. Tell us about your education and most important things you learnt growing up.

My Name is Mweemba Ntembe. I was born in Zambia 8th December 1990. I spent the majority of my childhood in Zambia, then moved to Botswana for two years before returning to Zambia.

At the age of 13 I moved to England, UK, to begin High school. Throughout high school, I was always interested in Business taking it as a major, in addition to business economics in higher education.

I then went on to study business with Marketing at Northumbria University.

After graduating, I worked in Marketing & Sales for two years before I decided to return home and began the process of starting my own company.

Do you think education in Africa motivates and equips African entrepreneurs?

I do not know about the whole of Africa but for my country this is not the case.

The education system here fails young entrepreneurs and research has cited that lack of entrepreneurial education is the reason why business people such as small-scale farmers fail to grasp the opportunities that are open to them.

Where did you get the idea for your business?

I got the idea when I visited Zambia. Several years ago, one of my family members owned a farm.

However, her produce was stored away and she was struggling to sell it because the locals weren't buying in bulk.

She also lacked the resources to make contact with buyers in Europe, Asia, and North & South America.

Even, if she had contacts with buyers outside Africa, she did not have the means to transport her harvest to these continents. This mean she could only trade locally which closed off major markets and the potential to increase her income.

This was a common issue among many of the small scale farmers.

I therefore decided to start a company which will help farmers in the same predicament come together as a cooperative in order to export their products, learn and support each other.

They would learn modern, sustainable and effective methods of farming such as saving seed to be used the next year, better methods of crop rotation and farming methods which do not cause harm to the environment whilst at the same time increasing yields.

How does your business model work?

The Panjiia Company brings smallholder Zambian farmers together as a cooperative, enabling them to trade to buyers in Asia, Europe and America by Panjiia.

The money which is made from trading is given back to the cooperative and the members share the gains equally.

The Panjiia company retains a percentage for its services. Part of this will go towards improving infrastructure, and the education of farmers.

We are trying to build a company which is aware of its stake holders and gives back to everyone involved and to the people of Zambia.

To summarize what the company stands for I can refer to our mission statement, which is: -

'Our aim and objectives is to provide a strong platform for African farmers to attain a decent market price for their produce.

Also to prevent abuse and exploitation of African farmers and to improve the overall quality of a farmer's standard of living and to assist in providing resources to enhance the level of their occupation. "

How do you attract customers?

We attract our customers through business to business direct marketing. This involves using direct forms of communication such as phone appointments, email and face-to-face meeting in order to close sales.

At the moment we are affiliated with a direct marketing company started by some fellow entrepreneurs a few years ago and it is our plan to use their skills.

What is the innovation in your business?

The business is structured to put the farmers at the centre of all activities. By bringing the farmers together they gain more control and increase their bargaining power with buyers.

Through this we believe that they are less likely to be underpaid. Our research has shown that smallholder farmers usually trade their crops at lower than market value prices due to desperation.

Also they can only trade locally amongst each other, making it a buyers' market.

Our company will focus strongly on social factors such as sponsoring and helping farmers cultivate their land in a more sustainable and profitable way.

What is the most fulfilling and rewarding part of what you have been doing?

The most fulfilling part is being able to help the people of my country. Very often cooperation's and governments profit whilst the small to medium sized farmer is left out. We thus plan on giving them a voice and ensuring they also get a profit.

What challenges have you faced during your time as an entrepreneur?

There have been many challenges; it's been a lot of hard work and when you can't see the materialized results sometimes it hard to keep going, but with a big dream like this it's also hard to give up.

Other challenges include arguments with family members as we spend more time working on the idea and are left with little time to socialize.

We have struggled to convince financial backers but we will push through.

What are your three most important things you had done for your success?

We are at the early stages but I believe that we will make this company successful. We are putting people first "help other improve their lives and success will find you".

My partner and I are dedicated to realizing this vision and it is something that speak to us wholly.

Has anyone mentored or inspired you?

After leaving University, I worked for two years for a Marketing company in London.

My boss was a man named Boyd Parker. He was a strong character who believed in a simple formula to success, which is find something you are passionate about, work hard and in no time you will find success.

Boyd Parker opened my eyes to the fact that success is not something reserved for the few but is something that we can all achieve if only we try.

Boyd Parker was not only my boss but a dear friend and a mentor. I would meet him early hours for breakfast and during this time he would give me some advice on business, life success and having a sense of purpose.

Boyd taught me that we should all treat others as we would like to be treated, it is our responsibility to be decent human beings and to use our time on earth to change the world and make other people's lives better.

He inspired me to pursue the Panjiia dream, to work with the people of Africa.

I realized that the agriculture sector was one which put the power back into the hands of the people themselves because it is a sector in which the farmers themselves have the potential to change their lives.

Other people that have inspired me include Richard Branson, Les Brown, Eric Thomas, Bill Gates, Steve Jobs and most important of all my mother.

The reason why these people have inspired me is because they started from nothing and in tough situations created something that had an impact not only in their lives but have truly changed the world and contributed to society.

How important has the mentor been for you?

My mentor was very important, when I first began doing Marketing. It was very tough but every evening I would meet with my mentor and he would give me lessons in all aspects of business.

Through my mentor I was able to learn the ins and outs of business, from Finance to Marketing, HR, Operations and selling. Not only was a mentor but a dear friend.

Mentors can be very important for entrepreneurs because business is a tough arena that's hard to manoeuvre.

Mentors, not only can provide the rock for those coming up but they can also offer valuable advice, motivation and plenty of inspiration.

How can you translate your experience into mentoring others?

In the future, I would like to be able to mentor young African entrepreneurs. Some of the people that have motivated me are motivational speakers such as Les Brown and Eric Thomas.

I believe they give so much to the world by helping people believe in their ability.

Some places in my country are so poverty stricken that people feel hopeless. It is in places like this that people can use a little motivation and a bit of self-belief with the knowledge that it doesn't matter how bad things are, you could always be successful.

What three advice do you have for other entrepreneurs?

Find something you love and enjoy doing; stick to it and success will come. Very often people get distracted by the prospects of money, fame etc.

However, if you don't enjoy what you are doing it very unlikely that you will succeed at it. So find what you love doing and stick to it.

It's going to be tough but carry on going, from working sales I have learnt that very often you will get the no, but if you carry on going that yes will eventually come.

There is no substitute for hard work, they say no pain no gain and I believe that holds truth especially when it comes to business.

What prospects do you see for your company?

In the future, I would love to see my company become one that uses it profits to help people, possibly a Foundation for young entrepreneurs.

I want to see my company be one that spreads into many industries and promotes the hiring of young people in my country who very often find it very hard to obtain jobs.

How important is innovation and innovators like you for the development of Africa?

Innovation is the key to the development of Africa because it is through innovation that any country can develop.

Innovative people bring new ideas to old formulas. In places such as my country, it seems business people have been going through the same circles and it's about time fresh minds brought something new to the table.

What industries and lucrative business areas do you think will provide future business opportunities for African entrepreneurs?

There is huge potential in the tech industries. Africa has plenty of innovative young minds in the tech sector.

However, they are not getting the support and exposure that they need. If there was a tech hub similar to Silicon Valley the possibilities are endless.

Farming also offers a good business prospects. For example, according to research by IFAD[12] in Zambia only 20% of the total arable land has been cultivated.

What this means is with help via funding smallholder Zambians have the potential to expand and there's also potential for others to go into the same industry.

Africa has the potential to be a powerhouse in the Agriculture industry.

In many ways it already is but its resources are not been used very effectively.

---

[12] The International Fund for Agricultural Development (IFAD), a specialized agency of the United Nations, was established as an international financial institution in 1977 as one of the major outcomes of the 1974 World Food Conference.

In the UK the government has set up farmers associations which support farmers financially. In addition, through education, these help farmers grow and expand by helping them export Worldwide. This is exactly what Africa/Zambia needs.

African governments and entrepreneurs should really put a lot more effort into promoting this industry.

Other industries include tourism, transport, education and health.

What support do you think African governments must give to young African innovators and entrepreneurs?

The government can definitely do a lot more to fund new startups. It is on their agenda to increase employment and yet they miss the fact that it is through promoting entrepreneurship that they can create jobs, because it is small businesses that hire people and as they grow, hire even more people.

They should create a support system which helps entrepreneurs and innovators financially and mentally; it's tough to be an entrepreneur and if they had a place they could go for advice this would help them immensely.

As well as financial help, the government should create institutions which bring them together so they can collaborate and help each other live their dreams.

For example, in England there is the bay business Centre. At this center, I was able to meet other entrepreneurs in sectors that I needed help; social media marketing, web design, logo design etc.

If you were President, what would you do or what would you change to encourage growth in entrepreneurship?

I would introduce an organization which focuses on entrepreneurs and helping them progress. There needs to be an institution that brings together entrepreneurs of all ages and help them achieve their dreams and goals.

As well as providing education the institution should be able to offer financial support, in a country such as the UK there are record number of new business and ideas every year because the governments here offer exactly such support.

Lessons Learned

What type of innovation?

This is an example of Service Innovation, specially innovation in the service process. If we look at the four dimensions of den Hertog model[13] , we find all of these in The Panjiia Company.

The four dimensions are as follows:

The Service Concept: Mweembe is organizing several activities or facets along the supply chain to provide a new service to Zambian farmers.

The Client Interface: Here we see innovation in the interface between Zambian farmers and buyers of their produce. Often times, the buyers are highly involved in the service production.

However, Mweemba has spotted a gap between the buyers and the suppliers- in this case the Zambian farmers.

The Service Delivery System: Mweemba is building services focusing on the linkages between the service provide (The Zambiam Farmer) and the clients.

Technological Options: Mweeba is building his services utilizing modern technologies.

The Source of his Innovation

---

13   Financial   Times/Lexicon.
http://lexicon.ft.com/Term?term=technology-eco-system
den Hertog (2000)

The source of his innovation is market inefficiency[1]. Due to a market inefficiency[14] a family member was not able to maximize her revenues.

What are the lessons?

An immediate lesson is that the agricultural sector is ripe for innovations along the supply and value chain.

Given the importance of this sector, such innovations could have a profound effect on the incomes of millions of small holders across the continent.

A further lesson is understanding where the problem lies along the supply chain. Mweemba has identified several factors that he believes he can solve.

Finally, we learn how important a mentor can be. Mweemba describes his mentor as "a rock" in his life.

What opportunities for further ideas or development of a new business?

---

14 A market anomaly (or market inefficiency) is a price and/or rate of return distortion on a financial market that seems to contradict the efficient-market hypothesis. The market anomaly usually relates to: Structural factors, such as unfair competition, lack of market transparency, regulatory actions, etc.

The agriculture sector is of vital importance in African economies. What Mweemba is doing in Zambia could be replicated in other countries.

We also believe that his platform can be leverage to specific farming sectors; for example diary producers.

Tips from the Authors

Transportation is a critical part of the agriculture supply chain.

We have no evidence that Mweemba has partnered with a transportation company.

We believe this of strategic importance and as such he should look for a long term partner in this area.

Erick Chrispin

Country: Tanzania

Company: Truemaisha

www.truemaisha.blogspot.no

Provides Management and Skills Development Training

Your background. Tell us about your education and most important things you learnt growing up.

I am Erick Chrispin, a Tanzanian by nationality holding a bachelor degree in Sociology and Anthropology from 2010.

My first business was selling my first book I wrote on Advanced Level Secondary school grammar. This business saw me joining and later becoming a People's director of Dar es Salaam University Entrepreneurship Forum.

In 2010, after my graduation, I joined the University of Dar es Salaam Entrepreneurship Center (UDEC) as a volunteer in the investor match making project done by BiD Network - a Dutch organization[15] .

----

15 The aim to increase economic development in emerging markets by provid-ing small and medium sized

After 8 months, I left my job with BiD and joined ActionAid Denmark, where I was employed in Dar Es salaam by their Global Platform Tanzania. This is a training for change center and my job was as a Social entrepreneurship course developer and trainer.

Prior to starting the job proper, I underwent an international Training of Trainers for change course held by ActionAid Denmark in Dar es Salaam.

In 2015 I founded the Tanzania Social Entrepreneurship Forum (TASEF), working as its chairman.

I am also an author of a personal development book titled "Tabia 5 za watu waliofanikiwa" (5 habits of successful people) from which I do motivational talks around Tanzania.

The most important things I learnt growing up are that our nation needs proactive young people who will take risk to create jobs for it to grow economically.

Business can never grow if one is not applying entrepreneurial principles like being creative and innovative, redefining challenges not being something to

---

enterprises (SMEs) access to capital and knowledge. http://www.bidnetwork.org/about/

run away from instead embrace and use them to your advantage.

We should stop believing in a poverty culture as many of us in African countries are being preached to for so long that we are poor.

It is easy to grow only if we are ready to synergize our different activities through partnerships.

Do you think education in Africa motivates and equips African entrepreneurs?

I don't think so.

What I see is that our education system only prepares future employees. The system is not giving students time to create and conceptualize new ideas; rather it forces students to cram notes for passing examinations.

This results in their low esteem when it comes to the job market. They do not become competitive hence the unemployment rate increases in our countries. As far as Tanzania is concern this is very high.

Where did you get the idea for your business?

Since I had been training people in leadership, management, Entrepreneurship and personal development for almost 4 years, I saw an opportunity for me to make it a business.

However, I was much motivated by my blog *www.truemaisha.blogspot.com* from which I had been writing articles.

I actually began to get people willing to pay me to teach them. From here the idea of establishing my business germinated.

How does your business model work?

In our company we run training in two different modes; we have our open training programs which people apply to attend and the next mode is our tailor made training programs which are tailored according to customer's need.

How do you attract customers?

We are always trying our best to be different in terms of charges and training methodology as well.

For instance, we charge minimal if a number of participants is large and they are from low economic class. In this case we offer our charges per group.

On the other hand, we charge higher and per individual if we are working with people of high profile.

What attracts more customers is our participatory methodology in trainings. In Tanzania, most trainers prefer "lecturing", but on our side we use more of facilitation since our philosophy is based on learning from experience.

As a result, our participants will always ACT, REFLECT and APPLY what they have learnt.

We also make sure we have a sustainable relationship with our customers by having a sustainable mentorship and follow-up system to our trained participants by observing their progress.

What is the innovation in your business?

We have come up with a program called *Human resource capacity building management* from which we never ask our customer to buy our training programs.

Instead, we ask them if they can allow us to discover a gap in their human resource performance.

We do so by conducting an almost free performance needs assessment.

We then share the results with our clients and they see what the gap is in their team. From the result and subsequent discussions, we develop a capacity building program.

After that we take time to follow-up and measure performance progress of their workforce; we measure a return on investment and develop a report for our client. This creates a sustainable relationship with our client since we become managers of their human resource capacity building process.

What is the most fulfilling and rewarding part of what you have been doing?

Seeing people's lives get transformed because of the training I have provided them, is the most fulfilling and rewarding part of what I have been doing.

I believe this to be my purpose in life, and for this reason I am so committed and persistent in what I am doing.

Regardless of a number of challenges I am facing, I have never given up because I always see people's lives change because of my work.

What challenges have you faced during your time as an entrepreneur?

The big challenge has been to build a new reputable company. Moving from freelance to full time, required that I restructure our training programs and start attracting new customers.

Always in business, people buy from whom they know and trust. This creates somewhat of a challenge to new business that has little experience serving in the market.

The next challenge has been financial resources to employ more support team. I thus found myself overworked and as a result effectiveness and efficiency became affected somehow.

However, all these challenges were critical factors for me to learn and grow my business

I also face a big challenge during registration of my business. In Tanzania, the system of registration is complicated and usually does not favor startups.

The process takes too long and the requirements are not centralized.

For instance, one should go to the business registration agency to register a business name or company, then leave and sometime travel to search for a Tax I identity number (TIN) somewhere else; then one will go somewhere else to search for a business license.

Most of these departments are bureaucratic and sometimes prone to corruption. The bureaucracy caused delays.

In my case, it took almost 5 months to be registered. Part of the problem is that there is no one stop shop for the registration process.

I do advocate that the process is centralized, which would allow startups to quickly get their companies going, hence grow our economy.

What are your three most important thing you had done for your success?

I have started my own company which I am working full time now ; I have written the best book which positively affects its readers and gives me a platform to teach, and I have managed to brand myself as a professional trainer which gives me more work online.

Has anyone mentored or inspired you?

Yes, I have a mentor for my business but also I have role models whom I admire and get inspiration from to move on every day.

How important has the mentor been for you?

My mentor has been so important to me since she always tell me the truth when I am doing wrong in my business; she always challenge me and I made my mind that I need to accept her challenges in order to grow.

As such, she acts as my mirror to see how I look like and discover where to correct my appearance and this makes me grow.

She always shares with me her experience in business which makes me learn.

How can you translate your experience into mentoring others?

I will always rely on my experience doing business to mentor others.

However, their questions to me will determine what I am going to advise and guide them.

Each business has its critical factors which must be addressed for it to work better.

I will always work hard to discover other people's critical factors and compare to how I resolved mine before mentoring others through such experience of mine.

In delivering my mentorship then I will write articles in my blog, write a book, speak and teach people directly or coach my mentee face to face.

Which African Entrepreneurs inspire you and why?

I am inspired by Eric Shigongo[16] a Tanzanian businessman since he rose from poverty to become the richest man in Tanzania. I love his processes of growing his businesses through helping other people grow too and for real it gives me energy most of the time.

I also get inspired by a great young African musician from Tanzania - Diamond Platnumz[17] - for me he is a

---

16 Eric Shigongo is an author, motivational speaker and media owner, as CEO of Global Publishers Ltd, publishes newspapers and books. The newspapers and books are available globally through the internet.

17 Nasibu Abdul Jumma (born 2 October 1989), popularly known by his stage name Diamond Platnumz (or simply Diamond), is a Bongo Flava recording artist and dancer from Tanzania. He is best known for his hit song "Number One". Diamond has won numerous

great entrepreneur. He is really working hard to succeed in his business and that is what inspires me to move on my business.

What three advice do you have for other entrepreneurs?

Entrepreneurship is a behavior one should generate from within so one need not to learn it from class instead associate with entrepreneurs to get practical experiences.

Entrepreneurs must define their challenges as what gives them businesses and they should expect to face and overcome challenges in their business lifetime.

---

awards at Channel O and the Prestigious HiPipo Music Awards. He performed at the Big Brother Africa 7 eviction show in May 2012 and also toured Europe, America and Asia. Diamond is considered influential among his fans especially Maria J, and is said to be the most loved and decorated Tanzanian artist at the moment. He is believed to be the highest selling Tanzanian artist of ringtones by mobile phone companies currently, as well as being among the artists earning the highest income in the African Great Lakes region's music industry. Also Diamond Platnumz holds a record of the highest paid artist in East Africa per Show Diamond platnumz was paid100 million Tsh in one show known as Tigo Kiboko Yao Concert his biggest steps currently was winning the MTV ema's best worldwide act.

Determination, working hard, concentration and persistence is what will make an entrepreneur achieve objectives.

What prospects do you see for your company?

I see my company to be an icon of personal transformation; first in Tanzania and Africa in the next 10 years.

How important is innovation and innovators like you for the development of Africa?

They are the only one who will change the look of Africa in terms of economic development.

Africa need people with an extraordinary mind, it needs people who are against dependency syndrome; African needs people that will recognize the plenty of opportunities and transform them into business to advance our economy.

What industries, and lucrative business areas do you think will provide future business opportunities for African entrepreneurs?

I think the technology sector is what should be a must in Africa. I believe that technology will develop more big investments in Africa.

Technological development open doors to many business opportunities since without technological development sometimes is very hard to see opportunities and the possibility to seize them when they are discovered.

By technology here I mean the modern resources to facilitate the processes of achieving some practical business objectives.

What support do you think African governments must give to young African innovators and entrepreneurs?

The governments need to create infrastructures and systems which leverage young African innovators and entrepreneurs to practice and start their innovations.

They need to simplify business formalization processes for startups, develop systems which will encourage incubation and mentorship to startup entrepreneurs.

Governments need to transform our education system and make it more participatory and practical just to encourage an enterprising mindset and culture to African students who are the future entrepreneurs.

If you were President, what would you do or what would you change to encourage growth in entrepreneurship?

I would process the transformation of our education curriculum at all levels so that it starts implanting entrepreneurship culture to kids from primary to university level.

I would also encourage more domestic business development and export economy to reduce dependence ratio.

To achieve this, I would involve our big and potential great minds within our country to think and lead different sectors instead of using irrelevant politicians.

Lessons Learned

What type of innovation?

This is another example of Service innovation. Eric has established his own training company. His innovation is his participatory methodology in training.

In Tanzania, most trainers prefer "lecturing", but Eric use more of facilitation since his philosophy is based on learning from experience so the participants will always ACT, REFLECT and APPLY what they learn. This is the innovation that has made his business stand out.

In addition, Eric has instituted what he calls a sustainable mentorship and follow-up system. This ensures that they are able to follow up their trained participants, offering advice whenever this is needed.

Further Erick has developed *Human resource capacity building management program* which is design to discover a gap in the human resource performance of a company.

According to Erick it is quite unique that his company carries out a needs assessment, and then share the result with the client. The need assessment shows what the gap is in the client company's team.

Eric then develops a capacity-building program for them which is highly tailored for such a gap.

The end result is that they go beyond providing training to becoming managers of the client's human resource capacity building process.

The Source of his Innovation

The sources for his innovation lies in the development of a skills training market on a globally and in Africa.

Added to his is his own experience as a trainer.

Finally his blog became a sort of ideas pool.

What are the lessons?

The real lessons learned in this story is how E. Crispin uses his mentor. Both him and his mentor have developed a bond, which he described as "his source" for growth.

Being an entrepreneur within teaching and learning is not easy, but Erik is coping despite the challenges. His experience, his book and his blog strengthen his offering.

In all this he wants to help his nation to build proactive young people.

To see people evolve and get their lives transformed is his purpose in life!

What opportunities for further ideas or development of a new business?

As the speed of technology changes and new knowledge emerge, Eric would find more opportunity to offer new skills to his clients.

We need entrepreneurship in our education curriculum at all levels. And also find good businessmen who wants to help building people and building the nation.

Politicians can`t do everything!

Tips from the Authors

Eric should consider utilizing online platform for his courses. We know that more and more education and training is shifting online.

One major advantage is that the user can train at their own pace and also at their own location.

The location is an important point. Currently, Eric is based in Tanzania.

As he has regional expansion plans, offering some of his training online will be key to his regional expansion.

Oswald Abioseh Dundas

Country: Sierra Leone

Innovator

Your background. Tell us about your education and most important things you learnt growing up.

My name is Oswald Abioseh Dundas. I am 24 years of age. I attended the Sierra Leone Grammar School where I attained my senior certificate exams (WASCE).

I later attended Silicon Pro were I am studying information technology (IT).

Growing up I learnt many things such as how to repair and properly maintain a phone, computer and other electronic devices. I also learn how to print t-shirts .

Do you think education in Africa motivates and equips African entrepreneurs?

I don't think education in Africa motivates African innovators and entrepreneurs but I will say it rather equips them in some ways.

For example, the commercial stream were you have to deal with business knowledge that can be implemented on the business and the science stream that teaches basic physics that can be applied in building a complex innovation project.

Where did you get the idea for your business?

The idea for my innovations was from comics, movies and with a gift from God. I have many other innovations such as rechargeable belt; a readable night glass.

However, the most outstanding one is my recent robot. This is a 5.4 feet tall human shaped robot name DOTNASSER.

I built it entirely by myself!

This robot has functions such as- taking a photo; recording a video and can say phrases such as "good morning" and "how are you".

I should mentioned that DOTNASSER can actually take photos and record videos at night with an installed web cameras.

DOTNASSER can move its head, arm a finger, waist and two legs.

However, DOTNASSER cannot walk because I still need financing to complete the legs.

Sierra Leone is not an advance country in terms of technology such as robots and all this is why my innovation is unique and it is the first in West Africa.

What is the most fulfilling and rewarding part of what you have been doing?

The most rewarding part of this is to prove that Africans have talent and that anything can be achieve only if we put our minds to it.

What challenges have you faced during your time as an entrepreneur?

My major challenge I face is the lack of finance to get appropriate tools and recommended parts for my projects.

What are your three most important thing you had done for your success?

Three most important thinks I did for success are; Trust God for wisdom knowledge and understanding; Ensure that I stay focus and determine to continue till the end no matter what, and use what I have to get what I need in term of materials.

Has anyone mentored or inspired you?

I don't have any mentor for now and I am inspired by problems around me.

Mentoring other will be like another challenge that I will have to face as I will meet people that will find it hard to learn and others might even be brilliant than I am. I have been inspired by innovators such as Kelvin Doe[18] and many others.

What three advice do you have for other entrepreneurs?

I will advise other young innovators to be original in what they do, be focus and not distracted by critics and to always dream big.

---

18 Kelvin Doe (born 26 October 1996 in Freetown), also known as DJ Focus, is a Sierra Leonean engineer. He is known for teaching himself engineering at the age of 13 and building his own radio station in Sierra Leone, where he plays music and broadcasts news under the name "DJ Focus." He was one of the finalists in GMin's Innovate Salone idea competition, in which Doe built a generator from scrap metals. Doe would constantly use discarded pieces of scrap to build transmitters, generators, and batteries, as well. As a result of his accomplishment, he received an invitation to the United States and subsequently became the youngest person to participate in the "Visiting Practitioner's Program" at MIT. His accomplishments were documented by @radical.media and presented on their corporate YouTube channel. When the video went viral, the story was picked up by CNN, NBC News, and The Huffington Post. Doe subsequently was a speaker at TEDxTeen and lectured to undergraduate engineering students at Harvard College. In May 2013, Doe signed a $100,000 solar project pact with Canadian High Speed Service Provider Sierra WiFi.

What support do you think African governments must give to young African innovators and entrepreneurs?

I think African governments can help young African innovators by providing facilities (labs) for gifted and talented people; provide funding for research and upgrade school to be doing basic robotic and electronics courses.

Organize competitions in art, singing, innovations etc to identify talented people.

If you were President, what would you do or what would you change to encourage growth in entrepreneurship?

If I was the president I will give scholarship to people who deserve them and pay more attention in the development of science and technology areas. I will open an institution that caters for gifted people in diverse talent.

Lessons Learned

What type of innovation?

This is an example of a New product innovation.

The first person to develop a 5.4 feet tall human shaped robot name DOTNASSER in Sierra Leone!.

This is truly an amazing achievement for a 24 year old, living in one of the poorest countries in the world, not to mention a very challenging city.

The city is often without electricity. His creativity and engineering skills are impressive.

The Source of his Innovation?

His education and the fact that with new knowledge he is able to build a robot.

This is also a story of curiosity. Oswald had few friends in his age group while growing up. In his own words, "sometimes I am alone and this offers me a chance to experiment".

I reached a point where I needed more money to buy things like material for experimenting on things such as battery and glue.

This was when I also began to repair cell phones and print t-shirts to earn an income.

What are the lessons?

We believe this young man is a perfect example of what one person can achieve with enough determination and passion.

To say, this is Africa's or West Africa's next big inventor is not far-fetched.

It is simply fantastic and inspiring to see what Oswald could do with so little.

Best lesson learned here is YOU CAN DO IT!!

What opportunities for further ideas or development of a new business?

There is an abundant field of opportunities for this young inventor.

With a 3 D printer, he could start an industrial design or even prosthetic company.

Tips from the Authors

Oswald is a very talented individual!

We strongly advise Oswald to pair up with someone (a person or a resource lab) so that he can be guided and helped to develop further.

It is also clear that he will need a mentor and get international exposure to nurture his talents further.

The Authors

Francis Stevens George

Francis Stevens George was born in Freetown, Sierra Leone. He graduated from the London School of Economics and Political Science with BSc Economics and International Relations (1989); has an MBA from the Norwegian School of Management (1993) and a Masters in Innovation, E-enterprise and Leadership (2005).

In the past 18 years, Francis has been a successful serial entrepreneur. He started 5 of his own companies; has been part of the start-up team of 3 companies; and has been a consultant/Manager for 3 early stage companies.

Francis has cross industry experience, having worked in primary, secondary, knowledge and Quinary industries. He has worked in small, medium, and large organizations in senior management roles and as a consultant.

His consulting work has included AMSCO (part of the World Bank Group), NORAD and The Foundation for Sustainable Development. In 2002, Francis was part of the UN ICT Task Force. Between 2001-2003 Francis ran workshops and courses in e-business and Innovation to a cross section of industry (Banking, Hospitality and Medical) in West Africa.

In 2005 Francis founded Innovation Africa, which aggregates news, research and tools on Innovation both within and from outside the continent.

Francis is an accomplish author having published several books-both fiction and non-fiction. He has also authored several papers on Business models, Leadership, Innovation and Technology.

Francis has lived in Norway since 1990. In 2016, he will lead the efforts of the Global Entrepreneurship Network in Sierra Leone.

Contact:

www.innosl.com,

www.innovationafrica.org

Twitter:@fsgthird

Thor-Erik Gulliksen

Since 1994, Thor-Erik has run workshops and courses in entrepreneurship, marketing, sales, custom care, personal development, coaching and mentoring. He has been a consultant in different companies and branches and also helping over 250 companies within Junior Achievement – Young Enterprise.

He is born in Norway. He has an International marketing and entrepreneurship education from the Norwegian School of Management, Catholic Institute of Business Administration (ICADE – Madrid, Spain) and ESADE Business School (Barcelona, Spain). Pedagogical

Education at University College of Southeast Norway and coaching and counseling from Oslo and Akershus University College of applied sciences.

Since 1999, he has worked with mentoring mostly between students and businesspeople. Over 500 people have attended one of Mr. Gulliksen mentoring programs. He is also mentor business people within business and personal development.

Mr. Gulliksen has more than 20 years experience, including management, marketing, educational and training.

He is also an author for two books about mentoring, and in the third book he collected 27 entrepreneurship histories from 16 different countries. And he has also authored several papers on Business Models, Strategy and how to survive the first two years in business.

Contact Details: www.mentorguru.info

Twitter: @mentorguru

Table of Index

A

Africa · 3, 5, 6, 7, 8, 9, 3, 9, 12, 14, 15, 17, 26, 27, 32, 33, 34, 35, 42, 43, 46, 47, 48, 50, 51, 55, 56, 60, 63, 64, 65, 74, 82, 84, 85, 88, 90, 97, 100
Africa market · 9
African country · 37
African Entrepreneurs · 12, 32, 45, 82
agricultural · 15, 16, 70
Agriculture · 34, 65
agriculture sector · 61, 70
agriculture supply chain · 71
America · 2, 54, 56, 82
angel investors · 18
applications · 16, 22, 52
arable land · 64
ARED · 1, 4, 7
Asia · 54, 55, 56, 82
assessment · 77, 87
Atlanta · 2
autonomous companies · 22

B

BOP · 1, 4
Botswana · 54
branding · 4
Brick and mortar · 6
bureaucratic · 7, 79

Burundi · 2, 3, 21
business · 5, 7, 8, 1, 2, 3, 4, 5, 6, 7, 8, 9, 10, 11, 13, 15, 17, 20, 21, 22, 23, 26, 27, 29, 30, 31, 33, 34, 35, 36, 37, 38, 39, 42, 43, 44, 45, 47, 48, 49, 50, 51, 53, 54, 55, 56, 57, 58, 60, 61, 62, 63, 64, 66, 67, 70, 72, 75, 77, 78, 79, 80, 81, 83, 84, 85, 86, 87, 89, 91, 97, 100, 102
business models · 17
buyers · 54, 55, 56, 58, 68, 69

C

capacity building program · 77
Capital · 31
clean water · 15
Companies · 6, 15, 16
competitors · 52
continent · 7, 13, 46, 47, 51, 70, 100
cooperative · 54, 56
core components · 22
corruption · 79
create value · 52
creativity · 52, 96
customers · 5, 19, 20, 30, 37, 43, 57, 76, 78

D

Denmark · 73

Developing countries · 9
digital advertisement · 4
digitalized world · 9
DOTNASSER · 91, 92, 96
dynamic offering · 19

E

economic · 9, 1, 73, 76, 84
economy · 5, 18, 80, 84, 86
eco-system · 19, 20, 68
education · 2, 3, 25, 26, 33, 41, 42, 54, 55, 57, 65, 67, 72, 74, 85, 86, 89, 90, 96, 101
electricity · 17, 34, 96
electronic devices · 90
energy sector · 17
engineers · 27
England · 54, 66
entrepreneur · 8, 11, 12, 23, 31, 32, 43, 59, 66, 78, 83, 84, 88, 93, 100
entrepreneurs · 5, 7, 8, 3, 5, 12, 13, 15, 17, 26, 27, 32, 33, 34, 35, 42, 43, 45, 47, 48, 49, 50, 52, 55, 58, 62, 63, 64, 65, 66, 67, 74, 83, 84, 85, 86, 90, 94, 95
entrepreneurship · 9, 4, 17, 26, 35, 42, 48, 66, 73, 86, 89, 95, 101, 102
Entrepreneurship · 5, 6, 8, 14, 17, 27, 72, 73, 75, 83, 101
environmental · 8, 22, 35, 38
Europe · 54, 55, 56, 82

F

farmers · 54, 55, 56, 57, 58, 61, 65, 68, 69
Farming · 64
finances · 17
food · 16
fragmentation · 9
franchise business model · 4, 22
franchisee · 5, 6
franchisees · 5, 6, 7, 8, 20, 24
Freetown · 25, 94, 100

G

global warming · 15, 16
globalized · 9
Grammar School · 90
greenhouse gases · 22

H

human resource · 77, 87

I

industries · 15, 34, 47, 63, 64, 65, 84, 100
infrastructure · 57
innovation · 5, 8, 9, 5, 6, 14, 15, 19, 20, 22, 30, 34, 37, 38, 43, 46, 49, 50, 58, 63, 68, 69, 77, 84, 86, 87, 88, 91, 92, 95

Innovation · 3, 7, 8, 14, 20, 36, 37, 49, 51, 63, 68, 69, 88, 96, 100, 101
innovation systems · 8
Innovative · 5, 64
innovators · 7, 8, 14, 17, 34, 35, 46, 48, 49, 52, 63, 66, 84, 85, 90, 94, 95
intelligent services · 4, 14
internet hot spot · 4
internet of things · 16
Italy · 26

K

Kenya · 2, 100
knowledge · 37, 62, 73, 89, 91, 93, 96, 100

M

Management · 25, 72, 100, 101
marketing · 30, 57, 58, 66, 101, 102
MBA · 26, 29, 31, 100
mentor · 10, 11, 23, 32, 39, 40, 44, 45, 53, 60, 61, 62, 70, 80, 81, 88, 93, 98, 102
mentoring · 11, 31, 44, 62, 81, 101, 102
methodology · 76, 86
Milan · 26
Milton Margai College of Education Science and Technology · 25
mobile money · 4, 6, 22
mobile phone · 21, 83

mobile solar kiosk · 1, 4, 5, 6, 21
money · 4, 8, 18, 28, 37, 39, 44, 48, 56, 62, 96

N

Namibia · 7, 41, 43, 45

O

organization · 52, 67, 73

P

paradigm shift · 36, 37
paradigm-based innovations · 36
partnerships · 53, 74
plastic waste · 25, 29, 30, 33, 36, 37, 38, 39
population · 16, 17, 28
poverty · 62, 74, 82
President · 17, 35, 48, 66, 86, 95
private sector · 18
product platforms · 22
product system innovation · 19
products · 16, 19, 20, 24, 33, 38, 43, 47, 50, 53, 56

R

raw materials · 38
recycling waste · 37

renewable energy · 17, 34, 35

research · 4, 16, 19, 21, 23, 46, 47, 55, 58, 64, 95, 100

Research and Development · 9

revenue · 5, 13, 38, 43

robot · 91, 96

Rwanda · 7, 1, 4, 5

S

scholarship · 29, 41, 45, 95

self-taught · 11

services · 4, 5, 6, 7, 16, 19, 20, 22, 24, 43, 47, 50, 51, 52, 53, 57, 69

Sierra Leone · 5, 7, 12, 25, 26, 27, 28, 34, 35, 37, 38, 39, 90, 92, 94, 96, 100, 101

Sierra Leonean · 25, 35, 94

Skills Development Training · 72

Small Medium Enterprise · 18

smallholder · 56, 58, 65

SME · 9, 17, 18

social · 9, 23, 41, 42, 43, 46, 49, 50, 51, 58, 66

social strategy · 51

solar energy · 22

sources of innovation · 8

South America · 14, 55

startups · 18, 66, 79, 80, 85

T

Tanzania · 7, 72, 73, 75, 76, 79, 82, 84, 87, 89, 100

tax incentives · 18

taxes · 7, 9, 17, 20

Technological Options · 69

technology · 5, 1, 4, 9, 13, 14, 15, 16, 17, 18, 37, 47, 50, 68, 85, 89, 90, 92, 95

Technology ecosystems · 22

Telecom · 15

The Client Interface · 68

The Service Concept · 68

The Service Delivery System · 69

theory · 19, 26

Transportation · 71

U

UK · 54, 65, 67

underutilized · 34

unemployment · 15, 75

UNIMAK · 25, 26, 29, 31

University · 2, 25, 26, 41, 45, 54, 60, 72, 102

USA · 2

V

venture capital · 18

W

waste management · 28, 29

waste recycling · 29

West Africa · 5, 92, 97, 100

WIFI internet · 5

workforce · 77

World Bank · 9, 100

Y

youth group · 28, 37, 39
youth unemployment · 15

Z

Zambia · 7, 54, 55, 57, 64, 65, 70
Zambian · 54, 56, 68, 69

Inspiring Quotes

"In today's world, paradoxically, it is the boldest action that is often the safest. Remaining where you are in a world that is changing so rapidly is in fact the most dangerous of all places to be in." – Hakeem Belo Osagie, Nigeria

"It's difficult to identify one specific reason or catalyst [for my success], but above all other things, I believe a strong sense of perseverance, always thinking big and aiming high, and of course positivity, has allowed me to realize my vision." – Ashish J. Thakkar, UAE

"You just have to believe that yes , there is a future in this country of ours and I can tell you right now, I don't believe we have even started doing anything in Nigeria because the opportunities are so ENORMOUS " – *Aliko Dangote   NIGERIA*